You Are Redeemed

Thirty Reminders of Your True Identity

Bridget A. Thomas

Scripture quotations are taken from the Holy Bible, New Living Translation, copyright ©1996, 2004, 2015 by Tyndale House Foundation. Used by permission of Tyndale House Publishers, Inc. Carol Stream, Illinois 60188. All rights reserved.

Visit the author's website at bridgetathomas.com.

Cover design and artistic design by Stacey Witkowski, StaceyWitkowski.com.
Edited by Brittany Clarke, brittclarke.com.

Disclaimer: The author of this book is not a licensed counselor. This book is not intended as a guide to diagnose any medical or psychological issues. If expert assistance is needed, please seek help from a healthcare provider or licensed counselor. This work is sold with the understanding that neither the author nor the publisher are held responsible for a perceived negative outcome as a result of the contents of this book.

ISBN-13: 978-1-7322020-1-6
ISBN-10: 1-7322020-1-X

Dedication

This book is dedicated to all Christians who need a reminder of their true identity in Jesus.

Introduction

I began writing this book in May of 2017, but I laid it aside to publish *Every Day is a Gift*. Finally after many months, I was able to turn my attention back to this book. I am so glad that things turned out the way they did. Much like our lives as Christians, this book has been redeemed, which also means that this book's new identity is much better than its old one.

If you are like me, then maybe you struggle with negative thoughts. Maybe you can easily feel down when life takes a wrong turn. Or maybe daily life is just plain hard. Anyone out there raising their hand? Whatever the case may be, I think you will be able to get some truth out of this book.

I wrote this book as much for myself as for you. I feel that Christians are missing the boat in so many situations in life. We allow obstacles to define our path. We let our past hold us hostage. And we never truly tap into our true identity in Jesus.

In this book you will find thirty short chapters, each focused on your true identity. There will be a Bible verse that corresponds with each chapter, because the Bible is our ultimate source of truth. Also with each segment you will find a prayer that coincides with the truth that you read for the day. The prayer is a starting place. Please feel free to expand in your own prayer time with the Lord. And finally, you will find a "Your Words Have Power" section. This is an affirmation that you can ponder throughout the day, based on the Bible verse.

I hope this book brings you a bit of inspiration and encouragement as you make your way through it. Now let's get started!

P.S. In the back of the book, I have included a special prayer for those of you who have not yet asked Jesus to come into your heart. If you are ready to take that step, I invite you to turn to the "Accepting Jesus into Your Life" section now. It will be the best decision you ever make!

1 ~ A New Person

This means that anyone who belongs to Christ has become a new person. The old life is gone; a new life has begun! – 2 Corinthians 5:17

Don't let the chains of your past hold you back any longer. If you have given your life to Jesus, then you are a new person. Yet too often we keep turning back. We pick up the chains and lock them around ourselves. It's as though we just can't believe that Jesus really did change us. We fall into our old patterns and bad habits all too quickly. Or sometimes we just keep looking over our shoulders at our old selves. You might have made mistakes in the past, but that is not who you are anymore. It is time to let it go and step into the shoes of the new person that you have become, thanks to Jesus.

Prayer: Father, help me grab hold of this new person that You created in me. I am so tired of walking around with my old sinful nature. I am tired of feeling like I have been restricted by my past. I am handing You all of my chains. Please help me to release them to You, so that I can step into the wonderful things that You have in store for me. In Jesus's name I pray. Amen.

Your Words Have Power: I am a new person.

2 ~ God's Masterpiece

*For we are God's masterpiece. He has created us
anew in Christ Jesus, so we can do the good things
he planned for us long ago. – Ephesians 2:10*

You are God's masterpiece. Let that soak into your heart
today. What an awesome feeling. It brings tears to my eyes
to think about that. The same One who created the entire
universe, created you. He created the planet that we live on,
He put all the stars in place, He formed the sun, and He
molded the moon. He placed the earth on an axis and set it
in motion. He sends the earth on a trip around the sun each
year. He told the tide when to come and when to go. He
shaped huge mountains and vast oceans. How magnificent
to think that this glorious God also created you. And just
like the beautiful flowers in a field or the outstanding colors
at sunset, you are His masterpiece.

Prayer: God, what a wonderful thing this is to know that I
am Your masterpiece. It leaves me speechless. Too often I
don't feel that I have any value. But from now on I want to

live with this knowledge in my heart, that I am Your masterpiece. In Jesus's name I pray. Amen.

Your Words Have Power: I am God's masterpiece.

3 ~ God's Thoughts About You Cannot Be Numbered

You saw me before I was born. Every day of my life was recorded in your book. Every moment was laid out before a single day had passed. How precious are your thoughts about me, O God. They cannot be numbered! – Psalm 139:16-17

Dear friend, whatever might be weighing on your heart today, hold onto these words: God saw you before you were born. He saw your whole life before you took your first breath. He thinks about you so much that His thoughts about you cannot be numbered. I hope that reflecting on these words can help you to let go of your past, your mistakes, and your regrets. God is not holding onto those things, so why are you? God loves you so much and He doesn't want you to live in despair one more day. He doesn't want you to live your life feeling lost. He loves you and He wants you to accept and treasure His love.

Prayer: God, I confess that I do let my failures bring me down. But I am laying that aside. It is amazing to think that Your thoughts about me cannot be numbered. Today I will hold onto Your love. In Jesus's name I pray. Amen.

Your Words Have Power: God's thoughts about me cannot be numbered.

4 ~ A Child of God

But to all who believed him and accepted him, he gave the right to become children of God. – John 1:12

If you have accepted Jesus into your life, then you are a child of God. Maybe somedays you feel like you are not valuable and you are less important than the people around you. Perhaps at times you believe that you just don't have what it takes to do great things for the Kingdom of God, get that job you want, or tackle whatever mountain is in front of you. Or it could be that growing up you didn't get love from your earthly parents. But there is good news. You have a heavenly Father who adores you. Allow the knowledge that you are a child of the Most High God to give you renewed strength today.

Prayer: Abba Father, thank You for this glorious gift. I am in awe when I think about the fact that I am Your child. But unfortunately, most days I forget my true identity. I forget that I am a child of the King. Thank You for adopting me into Your family. In Jesus's name I pray. Amen.

Your Words Have Power: I am a child of God.

5 ~ A Spirit of Power, Love, and Self-Discipline

For God has not given us a spirit of fear and timidity, but of power, love, and self-discipline. – 2 Timothy 1:7

I know life can be difficult. We all face different trials in our lives. Some days we might want to give up. The mountain might seem too hard to climb. Fear can be crippling, but we cannot allow fear to rule our lives. When we became Christians, God gave us a spirit of power, love, and self-discipline. This spirit can help us climb that mountain. We might only take one small step at a time, but this will get us to the finish line. This spirit can help you to overcome whatever you may be facing today. Allow God to help you face that giant.

Prayer: Lord, there are times when I get weary with life. It is not always easy to navigate. And I allow fear to hold me back. Help me to remove fear from my life. I want to live with the spirit that You have given me: the spirit of power, love, and self-discipline. In Jesus's name I pray. Amen.

Your Words Have Power: I have a spirit of power, love, and self-discipline.

6 ~ Your Old Self Has Been Crucified With Christ

My old self has been crucified with Christ. It is no longer I who live, but Christ lives in me. So I live in this earthly body by trusting in the Son of God, who loved me and gave himself for me. – Galatians 2:20

Maybe when you became a Christian, nothing seemed to change. Perhaps you still lived life like before. Or maybe you did change, but not completely. It could be that from time to time you still see your old self appear. Whatever it is, know that God doesn't want to see us bound by pain, suffering, fear, addictions, emotions, pride, perfectionism, insecurities, doubts, worries, regrets, or anything else. There is only one true answer that will help you overcome this: Jesus. When you became a Christian, your old self died on the cross with Jesus. Your new self doesn't have to live by your old standards. It is time to let go of your old self.

Prayer: God, I confess that sometimes I still see things in myself that I do not like. My old self seems to taunt me. I am tired of trying to fight it on my own. I am laying down my old self at the foot of the cross. Please take this burden from me and help me to live a new life. In Jesus's name I pray. Amen.

Your Words Have Power: My old self has been crucified with Christ.

7 ~ The Spirit Who Lives in You

But you belong to God, my dear children. You have already won a victory over those people, because the Spirit who lives in you is greater than the spirit who lives in the world. – 1 John 4:4

It is difficult for a Christian to walk on the path of everyday life. The truth is that we live in a fallen world. Unfortunately, we will encounter adversity and hardships. We will deal with people who do not agree with us and are quick to judge us. We will also deal with our own self-doubts and insecurities. Life won't always be easy. But when you feel like it is you against the world, remember this: the Spirit that is in you is greater than the spirit that is in the world. And nothing can stop that Spirit. So keep pressing forward. Don't give up. You have what it takes living inside you.

Prayer: Father, it is true that sometimes I allow life to bring me down. Walking out the door of my home can be scary and depressing some days. But I know that when I became a Christian, Your Spirit came to dwell inside of me. And that is greater than anything I will face in this world. In Jesus's name I pray. Amen.

Your Words Have Power: The Spirit that lives in me is greater than the spirit that lives in the world.

8 ~ You Can Do All Things Through Christ Who Gives You Strength

For I can do everything through Christ, who gives me strength. – Philippians 4:13

Whatever obstacle you might be facing today, allow this verse to give you renewed power. I know life can be hard. When we became Christians, it didn't mean all of our troubles would disappear. But it did mean that we now have the one and only King of Kings on our team, going to bat for us. And that makes all the difference in the world. I honestly don't know how anyone can step out their door without having God by their side. But as Christians, we have this certainty to hold on to. And this will help turn any situation around.

Prayer: God, thank You so much for being by my side every day. Thank You for giving me the strength I need to face the day in front of me. I cannot face it on my own, but knowing that You are with me gives me the ability to press forward. In Jesus's name I pray. Amen.

Your Words Have Power: I can do all things through Jesus, who gives me strength.

9 ~ A Gift of Peace

"I am leaving you with a gift – peace of mind and heart. And the peace I give is a gift the world cannot give. So don't be troubled or afraid." – John 14:27

Peace. What a powerful word that is. Picture in your mind a person standing in the midst of chaos. There is havoc all around this person, but he is at peace. He is calm, despite all of the pandemonium he sees. This truly is a gift, just as Jesus said it was. Jesus walked this earth, so He knew the troubles we would face in this lifetime. He also faced many trials while on earth. But He always kept peace inside of Him, no matter what was going on around Him. And He has passed that same peace on to us. But we have to accept the gift that was given to us. He is holding it out in His palm. We need to accept it in order to be able to live in the same peace that Jesus did.

Prayer: Abba Father, I confess that many days I do not live with this peace inside of me. But I long to! Unfortunately, I allow day-to-day adversities to steal my peace. But right here and right now, I commit to changing that. I realize many of the hardships that come my way are put there by the enemy. He is the one who wants to steal my peace. But I will not allow that to happen any longer. Starting today, I am going to harbor the gift of peace that Jesus gave me. In Jesus's name I pray. Amen.

Your Words Have Power: Jesus has given me a gift of peace.

10 ~ Chosen

"You didn't choose me. I chose you . . ." – John 15:16

Sometimes in life we feel overlooked or even discarded by others. We go about our lives doing the best we can, yet at times we still feel like no one notices us or that no one cares about us. But the Bible verse above gives us a precious thought. We have been chosen. Those words warm my heart, and I hope they warm yours too. It feels good to know that our almighty God chose us. Imagine the Creator of the universe looking down at Earth. He sees billions of people scattered across the face of the planet. Yet in the midst of all those people, He not only sees you, but He also chose you.

Prayer: Heavenly Father, knowing that You chose me makes me smile. Some days I feel invisible and ignored. But knowing that You see me and chose me fills my heart with joy. Thank You! In Jesus's name I pray. Amen.

Your Words Have Power: God chose me.

11 ~ Appointed

". . . I appointed you to go and produce lasting fruit,
so that the Father will give you whatever you ask
for, using my name." – John 15:16

Many times in life we can feel like we have no purpose. We just go about our average day-to-day activities feeling as though we are not making an impact. But the verse above tells us that we have been appointed. This means that we do have a purpose. Our lives do have meaning. These words truly make me happy because for many years I felt like my life did not have any significance. If you have ever felt that way, please know that this is a lie from the enemy. You are important. And the things you do at home, at work, at church, or wherever you might go today will leave a legacy.

Prayer: God, I do want to live a life of value. I want to know I made a diffcrence in this world, all for Your glory. Please help me to boldly walk the path that You have laid out in front of me. In Jesus's name I pray. Amen.

Your Words Have Power: God appointed me to go and produce lasting fruit.

12 ~ The Salt of the Earth

"You are the salt of the earth. But what good is salt if it has lost its flavor? Can you make it salty again? It will be thrown out and trampled underfoot as worthless." – Matthew 5:13

The Bible verse above is a powerful one. It illustrates the impact we Christians have on those around us. When you have a meal without salt, it might be dull. But once you add salt, now your meal has some bang to it. The flavor is instantly enhanced. This is the effect we should have as well. We should leave an impression on the world by the way we live. Also, before the world had refrigerators, salt was important because it was used to preserve food. Take a look around you and you will see many areas of life that have been spoiled. Everywhere we turn, we see corruption and immorality. As Christians, we can help preserve godliness and integrity. As you go about your day today, remember that you are the salt of the earth.

Prayer: Lord, I want to be the salt of the earth that Jesus talked about. I want to leave a positive impact on those around me. Please help me to step out in bold faith today and to be a positive influence on everyone I encounter. In Jesus's name I pray. Amen.

Your Words Have Power: I am the salt of the earth.

13 ~ The Light of the World

"You are the light of the world – like a city on a hilltop that cannot be hidden. No one lights a lamp and then puts it under a basket. Instead, a lamp is placed on a stand, where it gives light to everyone in the house. In the same way, let your good deeds shine out for all to see, so that everyone will praise your heavenly Father." – Matthew 5:14-16

What a beautiful thought. You are the light of the world. I really love this verse because it gives us hope. In a dark world, we can bring light to those around us. In a depressing world, we can bring joy. In a dead world, we can bring life. In a cruel world, we can bring goodness. As Christians, we have a lot of power. But we have to tap into it. As you go about your day today, give extra thought to the things you say and do. Are you leaving a valuable imprint behind? Are you a shining light in a dark world?

Prayer: Heavenly Father, I long to be this person that Jesus talked about. I want to be a shining light for Your Kingdom. Whether I am at home, work, or even the grocery store, I want my light to shine. That is what life is all about, spreading light to those around us, all for Your glory. Please help me to be this person. In Jesus's name I pray. Amen.

Your Words Have Power: I am the light of the world.

14 ~ Rest

Then Jesus said, "Come to me, all of you who are weary and carry heavy burdens, and I will give you rest." – Matthew 11:28

Life can often leave us feeling pretty empty. We trudge through our days, just trying to get by. Sometimes things in life perk us up: the upcoming weekend, the next vacation, the holidays. However, many times between those peaks, we drag through the valleys of life. But it's not supposed to be that way. Jesus came so that we might have life and have it in full. He doesn't want us to just go through the motions. He wants our days to be filled with meaning, purpose, and joy. But how do we grab hold of that? By resting in the Lord and giving Him our troubles. We keep a tight fist around everything. We think that if we are in control, then we can make sure that everything will go smoothly. But trying to control every single thing can wear us out. Hand it all over to God and allow Him to be the King in your life. You can trust God to work things out. And then you will be able to rest in His peace.

Prayer: Lord, I confess that most days I do feel like I am just going through the motions. Life has left me feeling tired and blah. I just try to make it through the day. But I don't want to live like that anymore. I want to experience Your peace and Your joy. Please help me to learn how to rest in You. In Jesus's name I pray. Amen.

Your Words Have Power: When I am weary, I can give my burdens to the Lord, and He will give me rest.

15 ~ The Potter and the Clay

And yet, O Lord, you are our Father. We are the clay, and you are the potter. We all are formed by your hand. – Isaiah 64:8

God wants to use each of us to create a beautiful work of art. But we have to be flexible, like the clay in a potter's hands. He is the artist, after all. The clay doesn't tell the artist how to proceed. The clay simply goes with the flow of the artist's inspiration. So when things in life don't go quite like you planned, remember that God is using everything to form an amazing masterpiece. One piece of the clay by itself might not look very pretty. But once it is all put together, it will be a stunning success. And if you allow God to use you for His glory, the piece of art created out of your life will be breathtaking.

Prayer: Father, I confess that I am not always good at allowing You to have control. When life starts spinning quickly, I get frustrated and upset. But I realize now that during those times. You may just be molding me into the unique individual that You want me to be. So from now on,

I will allow You to be the potter in my life. In Jesus's name I pray. Amen.

Your Words Have Power: I am the clay, and God is my potter.

16 ~ God Sees Your Heart

But the Lord said to Samuel, "Don't judge by his appearance or height, for I have rejected him. The Lord doesn't see things the way you see them. People judge by outward appearance, but the Lord looks at the heart." – 1 Samuel 16:7

The verse above comes from the Old Testament when Samuel was looking for the next king of Israel, who was David. This verse is such a heart-warming view of God. In today's culture, people are quick to judge and label each other. Often times we are misunderstood. And many of us Christians feel like we just don't fit in. All of this can bring us down. But I am learning more and more, that as a Christian, it is a good thing to not fit in with the world. So I hope this verse gives you a new perspective. Because the truth is that no matter how you feel about yourself and no matter how others feel about you, God sees you and He sees your heart. Let the beauty of this verse seep into every deep wound that you may carry.

Prayer: God, thank You for seeing my heart. Thank You for looking deep within at the things that really matter. Many people only look at the surface, but You have a way of seeing the hidden layers. Thank You. In Jesus's name I pray. Amen.

Your Words Have Power: People judge by outward appearances, but the Lord looks at the heart.

17 ~ The Holy Spirit is With You

"But when the Father sends the Advocate as my representative--that is, the Holy Spirit--he will teach you everything and will remind you of everything I have told you." – John 14:26

When Jesus walked this earth, people flocked to Him. They knew that there was an amazing power inside of Him. Sometimes I think of how wonderful it would have been for those people to meet Jesus face-to-face. However, the truth is, you and I have an advantage over them. We get to have the Holy Spirit with us all day, every day. When we became Christians, He came to dwell inside of us. What an awesome gift that is. But I know a lot of times we forget that we have access to the Holy Spirit anytime we need Him. We forget that God is right there to guide our steps. So for today, keep this in the forefront of your mind. In everything you say and do, seek the Holy Spirit's guidance.

Prayer: Lord, what an amazing gift You have given me. Daily life can be trying at times. But when I remember that the Holy Spirit is with me every single moment, I am in awe. Thank You, Lord, for being with me at all times. In Jesus's name I pray. Amen.

Your Words Have Power: The Holy Spirit is by my side.

18 ~ God Will Continue His Good Work Within You

And I am certain that God, who began the good work within you, will continue his work until it is finally finished on the day when Christ Jesus returns. – Philippians 1:6

Whatever you are facing today, I hope this verse gives you hope. Perhaps you have a dream that seems just out of reach. Or maybe your life has hit a dead end. Whatever the case may be, whatever it is that you are up against, don't let it bring you down. There is always hope. Even when you have a mountain in front of you, remember that God is still on the throne. Just call on Him and He will be there. He is always faithful and He will complete the good work within you. So whatever it is that you are dealing with, hand it over to Him.

Prayer: Heavenly Father, thank You for giving me hope. Today I was worried about many things that I am facing and many trials in my life. But I am handing them over to You. Thank You, Father. In Jesus's name I pray. Amen.

Your Words Have Power: God, who began the good work within me, will continue His work.

19 ~ Christ's Ambassador

So we are Christ's ambassadors; God is making his appeal through us. We speak for Christ when we plead, "Come back to God!" – 2 Corinthians 5:20

As a Christian, you are Christ's ambassador. That is a very powerful position. You represent Jesus everywhere you go, in everything you do, and in all the words you speak. Every day you will encounter people who are lost. And you just might be the only reflection of Jesus that those people will see in the course of their day. Like a boat in the ocean, you have the power to start a wave. You can turn someone's day or life around. You can bring a smile to someone's face. And hopefully, you can also bring Jesus into their heart. For today, with each person you encounter, remember that you are representing Jesus.

Prayer: Lord, I want to be a good ambassador for Your Kingdom. I know at times I get wrapped up in my own troubles and I don't always say or do the right things. So please help me to turn this around. Give me the strength and courage to represent Jesus well. In Jesus's name I pray. Amen.

Your Words Have Power: I am Christ's ambassador.

20 ~ Forgiven

But if we confess our sins to him, he is faithful and just to forgive us our sins and to cleanse us from all wickedness. – 1 John 1:9

Forgiveness can be a tough subject for many of us. We tend to hold grudges against others who have hurt us, and often we find it hardest to forgive ourselves for the mistakes we have made. In a way, this is a good thing. It shows that we truly have a repentant heart. But sometimes we take it too far and beat ourselves up for far too long. And in the back of our minds, we might also feel as though God is still holding our pasts against us. But if you have confessed your sins to God, He has forgiven you. Accept God's forgiveness, It is a free gift that He is happy to give to us, thanks to Jesus. It is time to let go of the past, put all of that behind you, and move forward into your future.

Prayer: God, I have been allowing my mistakes to linger in my mind. I have not forgiven myself, and I have not fully accepted Your forgiveness. But I am tired of allowing those things to rule me. I want to let them go once and for all. I thank You for the gift of forgiveness. I thank You for what Jesus did on the cross for me and my sins. Starting today I will accept Your forgiveness and not allow my past to reign over my life anymore. In Jesus's name I pray. Amen.

Your Words Have Power: When I confess my sins, He is faithful and just to forgive me.

21 ~ Nothing Can Separate You from God's Love

And I am convinced that nothing can ever separate us from God's love . . . – Romans 8:38

What an uplifting verse this is. No matter what we go through in life, no matter what mistakes we have made, no matter what lies ahead of us, nothing can ever separate us from the love of God. When I read this verse, it helps calm my fears. It diminishes my worries. When we look at our problems in life, they often appear monumental. But we are looking at them from a human perspective. God's perspective is completely different than ours. All in one view, He can see the whole story from beginning to end. And no matter what we are going through, God and His love are right there with us, every step of the way.

Prayer: Abba Father, thank You so much for Your love. Thank You for this reassuring verse. No matter what I face today, I will seek strength from You and Your love. In Jesus's name I pray. Amen.

Your Words Have Power: Nothing can ever separate me from God's love.

22 ~ Created in God's Own Image

So God created human beings in his own image. In the image of God he created them; male and female he created them. – Genesis 1:27

The Bible is filled with so many incredible verses, from beginning to end. And we see in the very first chapter that we were created in God's own image. Perhaps there are features about yourself that you do not like. Or maybe there are things about your life that you wish you could change. But the truth is that you are a beautiful creature, created in God's image. How remarkable it is to think that you were created in God's own image. So whatever it is that you don't like about yourself, let it go and hold onto this truth.

Prayer: Father, it amazes me to think that I was made in Your own image. When I look in the mirror, I often see things that I do not like. Every day it seems I criticize myself for different reasons. And I am sorry that I have gotten into this habit. From now on, I will hold onto the truth that I have been made in Your own image. In Jesus's name I pray. Amen.

Your Words Have Power: I was created in God's own image.

23 ~ Adopted into God's Family

God decided in advance to adopt us into his own family by bringing us to himself through Jesus Christ. This is what he wanted to do, and it gave him great pleasure. – Ephesians 1:5

Did you know that when you became a Christian, you were adopted into God's family? If you came from a broken family, you don't have to let that weigh you down any more. You are a part of God's family. And even if you came from a loving earthly family, this verse should still give you a warm feeling. You are now a part of the finest family there is. But what is even more amazing is that last part of this verse. Not only did God adopt you into His family, but it gave Him great pleasure to do so.

Prayer: Abba Father, thank You for adopting me into Your family the moment I accepted Jesus into my heart. It warms my heart to know that You wanted to adopt me and

You took pleasure in adopting me. Thank You so much for Your unending love. In Jesus's name I pray. Amen.

Your Words Have Power: God adopted me into His own family.

24 ~ The Mind of Christ

For, "Who can know the Lord's thoughts? Who knows enough to teach him?" But we understand these things, for we have the mind of Christ. – 1 Corinthians 2:16

When you gave your life to Jesus, you gained the mind of Christ. This means that you now agree with Him on spiritual matters. You stand for the things He stands for. You can see things from His perspective. But one important piece to the puzzle is that you now have discernment as well. Many Christians feel like they don't hear from God. But God is always there, speaking to us and guiding us. When you get a bad feeling in the pit of your stomach, it could be God steering you down a different path. When you are trying to make an important decision, God will give you peace about the correct way to go. It is crucial that you stop and seek His wisdom first, and He will be there to direct your steps.

Prayer: Lord, thank You for giving me the mind of Christ. Thank You for helping me to see things from Your perspective. And thank You for giving me discernment and leading me on the right path. In Jesus's name I pray. Amen.

Your Words Have Power: I have the mind of Christ.

25 ~ God Hears Your Prayers

And we are confident that he hears us whenever we ask for anything that pleases him. – 1 John 5:14

Have you ever wondered if God hears your prayers? Let me tell you that He does. And the Bible verse above confirms this. God hears your prayers. He hears every single word. Prayer is such a powerful tool we have to communicate with our Father in heaven. We can talk to Him about everything that is weighing on our hearts. It might seem at times He does not hear you, but He always does. He loves when we come to Him in prayer. He loves having that open relationship with us. We are His children and He enjoys when we want to interact with Him. So bring the things that are on your heart to Him today and trust that He hears you.

Prayer: God, thank You for hearing my prayers. I admit that at times I do wonder if You hear me or not. But You are a sovereign God, so of course this means that You do hear all of my prayers. I love that I can bring my heart to You and You will listen. In Jesus's name I pray. Amen.

Your Words Have Power: God hears my prayers.

26 ~ Righteous Through Faith in Christ

. . . I no longer count on my own righteousness through obeying the law; rather, I become righteous through faith in Christ. For God's way of making us right with himself depends on faith. –
Philippians 3:9

When we put our faith and trust in Jesus, that is the moment when we become right with God. As soon as we accept Him, we become blameless. Too often we try to keep doing good works in order to give ourselves value. I agree that it is wonderful to do good things out of love for our Savior. But we should not do those good things to make ourselves more virtuous. If you have accepted Jesus, you cannot become any more virtuous or more righteous than you already are. God cannot love you any more because He already loves you beyond measure. You are beloved. You are adored. You are cherished. You are treasured.

Prayer: Father, thank You so much for all the love that You bestow upon me each and every day. I want to soak it up and really know and feel how much You love me. Too often I doubt Your love and think that I have to work for it. Please help me to fully understand and absorb Your love for me. In Jesus's name I pray. Amen.

Your Words Have Power: I have become righteous through my faith in Jesus.

27 ~ God Will Hold You Up

"Don't be afraid, for I am with you. Don't be discouraged, for I am your God. I will strengthen you and help you. I will hold you up with my victorious right hand." – Isaiah 41:10

If you are facing something difficult today, please tuck this verse into your heart. Sometimes we face difficulties that seem just too hard to overcome. But there is good news. No matter how big the giant in front of you is, God is with you. No matter how daunting the obstacle in front of you is, you don't have to be discouraged. If you feel weak, He will strengthen you. Whatever you are facing, He will help you. When you are ready to fall, He will hold you up. This is a powerful promise that can help you face any trouble you might encounter in life.

Prayer: Thank You, Lord for this promise. Sometimes the things that I face in life seem unbearable, but I know that I can face anything with You by my side, strengthening me, and holding me up with Your victorious right hand. In Jesus's name I pray. Amen.

Your Words Have Power: I will not be afraid or discouraged, for God is with me. He will strengthen me and help me. He will hold me up with His victorious right hand.

28 ~ Clean as Snow

"Come now, let's settle this," says the Lord. "Though your sins are like scarlet, I will make them as white as snow. Though they are red like crimson, I will make them as white as wool." – Isaiah 1:18

Do you feel broken when you think about your past? Once we accept Jesus, it no longer matters what we did in the past. Jesus has taken our dirty, sinful selves and washed them clean. We are now as white as snow. All the stains are gone. All the blemishes have disappeared. We have become immaculate. What a glorious feeling to know that all of our sins are washed away. Sit and think about that for a moment. This one thing shows just how much God loves us. He took all of our dirt and grime and made us spotless and sparkling.

Prayer: God, because of you, all of my sins have been carried away in the current. And I am now clean and spotless. Thank You for washing away my sins. Thank You for making me as white as snow. I am so overwhelmed by this amazing act that You did for me. And I am so thankful for Your love. In Jesus's name I pray. Amen.

Your Words Have Power: God has removed my sins and made me as white as snow.

29 ~ Free

So if the Son sets you free, you are truly free. – John 8:36

As Christians, we don't have to be slaves to sin anymore. We don't have to keep falling into the same destructive patterns. We don't have to live in fear anymore. We don't have to hold onto our anger another moment. We don't have to let pride rule our lives. We can finally find the peace that surpasses all understanding. We can walk through life with confidence. We can allow the joy of the Lord to be our strength. Old habits may still come to the surface, but when they do, we have a decision to make. Will we let them continue to rule our lives? Or will we lay them down at the foot of the cross? This is something we might need to do over and over again. But it gets easier each time!

Prayer: Father, thank You for offering me true freedom. I have tried to handle things on my own for too long, and as a result, I have imprisoned myself. But I am going to allow You to take over, and unlock the door. I realize now that through You I will finally be able to be free. And this freedom is sweeter than anything I could have imagined. In Jesus's name I pray. Amen.

Your Words Have Power: I am truly free!

30 ~ God Rejoices Over You

"For the Lord your God is living among you. He is a mighty savior. He will take delight in you with gladness. With his love, he will calm all your fears. He will rejoice over you with joyful songs." –
Zephaniah 3:17

As we wrap up our thirty days together, I want to leave you with one of the most beautiful Bible verses. Allow this to soak into your heart all throughout the day. Let's go through each part of this Scripture piece by piece.

"For the Lord your God is living among you." This means God is with you every single moment of every single day. His presence is always there with you, no matter what you are going through.

"IIe is a mighty savior." How reassuring it is to know that He is there to save you. This should calm all your anxiety.

"He will delight in you with gladness." And He takes delight in you. Some days you might feel like you are worthless. But this one line proves that all of those negative thoughts and feelings are a lie from the enemy. The Most High God delights in you!

"With his love, he will calm all your fears." What a precious thought this is. Not only does God love you, but with His love, He will calm all your fears.

"He will rejoice over you with joyful songs." Wow! Can you imagine your heavenly Father singing over you? What a delightful thought!

Prayer: Dear Father, I truly needed to hear these words today. At times I feel down. The world around me can be depressing, and I allow all of my worries to build up inside. But all of those things fade away when I hear how much You love me. Thank You so much for Your love and for always being there for me. In Jesus's name I pray. Amen.

Your Words Have Power: God takes delight in me with gladness. With His love, He will calm my fears. He will rejoice over me with joyful songs.

Accepting Jesus into Your Life

Do you have a personal relationship with God? If not, then I invite you to begin one today. I promise you that you will not regret it. Having a relationship with God will bring comfort and peace into your life.

But having a relationship with God, starts with accepting Jesus. The Bible says that we are all sinners and fall short of the glory of God (Romans 3:23). We all deserve to perish (Romans 6:23). And there is nothing we can do on our own to achieve salvation (Ephesians 2:9).

But the good news is that "If you openly declare that Jesus is Lord and believe in your heart that God raised him from the dead, you will be saved" (Romans 10:9). This is because Jesus paid the price that we could never pay. He died for all of our sins. He took them on Himself so that we might have eternal life. Then three days after Jesus's death, He rose from the dead. This ultimately defeated death and gave us the hope of salvation.

A life with Jesus by your side can be so freeing. Every day we struggle with the weight of the world on our shoulders. But it doesn't have to be that way. We can accept Jesus into our hearts, and let God handle our troubles. If you believe this, I invite you to pray this prayer now:

Lord Jesus, I ask You to please forgive me of my sins. I believe that You died on the cross for me and rose from the grave three days later. I can never thank You enough for paying my sin debt. Thank You for hearing my prayer. Thank You for Your unconditional love. I am ready to hand my life over to You. I am ready to walk in Your strength and power. I am ready for You to be the center, purpose, and meaning in my life. I am ready for You to be my Lord and Savior. In Jesus's name I pray. Amen.

If you prayed this prayer, congratulations on your new life! I would love to hear from you. Please contact me at bridgetathomas.com/contact/.

Acknowledgements

First I want to thank Jesus. Without Him, nothing in this book would be true. We would not have the gift of salvation, we would not be new creatures, and we would not be free. Thank You, Jesus, for all You have done for us.

A big thank to my husband, Mickey. You have been by my side every step of the way. And even though my writing has taken time, you are still patient and encouraging along this journey. I love you forever!

Many thanks to my parents and my sisters who make the best cheerleaders! Thank you for all of your support and inspiration. I love you guys!

Thank you to my cover designer, Stacey. You continue to be a blessing to me with each project. I don't know where I would be without your ideas and creativity.

Thank you so much to my editor, Brittany. I very much appreciate your expertise and guidance.

And a big thank you to you, the reader! I am deeply grateful to have you read this book. I hope and pray that it has been a blessing to you.

About the Author

Bridget's passion is to help people learn to live freely in Jesus. She feels that Christians who have been set free, still live as though they are trapped, and her calling is to motivate Christians to break out of those chains. Bridget knows that she needs a whole lot of grace from Jesus, every single day. And she encourages others to find that grace as well.

Bridget loves reading in her spare time, and is a fan of classic literature. She enjoys traveling, crocheting, and watching college baseball and softball games. And she is particularly fond of looking for black bears in the Great Smoky Mountains. Bridget lives in Florida with her husband.

For more information or to contact Bridget, please visit her website at bridgetathomas.com.

www.ingramcontent.com/pod-product-compliance
Lightning Source LLC
Chambersburg PA
CBHW060148050426
42448CB00010B/2349